ROCKFORD PUBLIC LIBRARY

3 1112 01646841 1

D1307187

J 598.71 MCD
McDougall, Jennifer.
Parrots

JUN 2 4 2009

ROCKFORD PUBLIC LIBRARY

Rockford, Illinois

www.rockfordpubliclibrary.org

815-965-9511

DEMCO

PARROTS

Jennifer McDougall

Grolier
an imprint of
■SCHOLASTIC
www.scholastic.com/librarypublishing

ROCKFORD PUBLIC LIBRARY

Published 2008 by Grolier
An imprint of Scholastic Library Publishing
Old Sherman Turnpike, Danbury,
Connecticut 06816

© 2008 Grolier

All rights reserved. Except for use in
a review, no part of this book may be
reproduced, stored in a retrieval system,
or transmitted in any form, or by any
means, electronic or mechanical, including
photocopying, recording, or otherwise,
without prior permission of Grolier.

For The Brown Reference Group plc
Project Editor: Jolyon Goddard
Copy-editors: Ann Baggaley, Leon Gray
Picture Researcher: Clare Newman
Designers: Jeni Child, Lynne Ross,
    Sarah Williams
Managing Editor: Bridget Giles

Volume ISBN-13: 978-0-7172-6276-2
Volume ISBN-10: 0-7172-6276-6

**Library of Congress
Cataloging-in-Publication Data**

Nature's children. Set 3.
    p. cm.
    Includes bibliographical references and
    index.
    ISBN 13: 978-0-7172-8082-7
    ISBN 10: 0-7172-8082-9
    1. Animals--Encyclopedias, Juvenile. 1.
    Grolier Educational (Firm)
    QL49.N384 2008
    590.3--dc22

                        2007031568

Printed and bound in China

PICTURE CREDITS

Front Cover: **Shutterstock**: Margita Braze.

Back Cover: **Alamy**: Arco Images; **FLPA**:
Jurgen and Christine Sohn; **Shutterstock**:
Eric E. Cardona; **Superstock**: Age Fotostock.

Nature PL: Aflo 37, Roger Powell 13, Lynn
M. Stone 21, Mike Wilkes 41; **NHPA**: Nick
Garbutt 42, 45; **Photolibrary.com**: Manfred
Pfefferie 46; **Shutterstock**: John Austin 30,
Jeff Carpenter 5, Catnap 9, Michael De
Gasperis 14, Nicola Gavin 10, 34, Su Hsing
Fang 26–27, Eric Isselee 4, Jakee 6, Philip
Lange 22, Lana Langlois 29, Xavier Marchant
18, Chen Wei Seng 2–3, 38, Mark Yarchoan
33; **Still Pictures**: BIOS/Klein and Hubert 17.

Contents

FACT FILE: Parrots

Class	Birds (Aves)
Order	Parrotlike birds (Psittaciformes)
Families	Parrots, macaws, and lories (Psittacidae) and cockatoos (Cacatuidae)
Genera	Many genera
Species	There are more than 350 species of parrots in the world
World distribution	Parrots can be found in all the tropical parts of the world
Habitat	Tropical forests and scrublands
Distinctive physical characteristics	Many parrots have brightly colored feathers; feet suited to climbing; tough, curved beak
Habits	Noisy birds that can mimic sounds and words; live a long time; often live in groups
Diet	Mostly seeds, nuts, and fruit; some also eat insects; lorikeets eat pollen and drink nectar

Introduction

Parrots are brightly colored, noisy birds. They are very widespread, living in the tropical forests across the world—from the Amazon of South America to the forests and scrublands of Australia. Parrots have a very strong, curved beak, or bill, that can crack the toughest nuts.

Humans have a close relationship with parrots that goes back more than 4,000 years. Parrots were a favorite pet of Roman emperors, and they are still popular pets today. They are among the most intelligent of birds and can mimic, or copy, human words. Parrots are very long-lived. Some parrots have lived to 100 years in **captivity**.

Large parrots are also called hookbills because of their curved beak.

Pet hyacinth macaws have been known to tear apart the metal bars of their cage with their strong beak.

Parrot Family

Parrots and parakeets are the most familiar members of the parrot family. But there are many other members of the family, including cockatoos, cockatiels, budgerigars (BUH-JUH-REE-GARS), lorikeets, lories, and lovebirds. There are more than 350 species, or types, parrots.

Parrots range in size greatly. The smallest parrot is the buff-faced pygmy parrot that lives in the forests of New Guinea, an island near Australia. It weighs about one-third of an ounce (10 g) and is about 3⅕ inches (8 cm) long from head to tail. It's so small that it could fit in the palm of a child's hand. The largest parrots are called macaws. These colorful birds live in the rain forests of Central and South America. The hyacinth macaw can grow up to 40 inches (1 m) from head to tail and weigh 3½ pounds (1.5 kg). This rare and magnificent parrot has cobalt blue feathers with a yellow chin and yellow rings around its eyes.

Parrotland

Most parrots make their home high up in trees in tropical forests. These forests occur in many places, including South America, Africa, Australia, Southeast Asia, and islands in the Pacific Ocean.

Not all parrots live in trees, though. Some species from Australia and New Zealand have lost the ability to fly. Because these birds did not have any natural **predators**, they were happy living on the ground. However, in the past couple of centuries, European settlers have introduced animals that attack these birds and they are now under threat of **extinction**. Other parrots, such as cockatoos and budgerigars live in the scrublands of Australia. The Andean parakeet survives in the cold climate of the Andes mountains in Chile, South America. There are no naturally occurring parrots in the United States. However, a few species, such as rose-ringed and monk parakeets and budgerigars, have escaped or been released and now live and breed there.

Rainbow lorikeets live in the north and east of Australia.

Parrots often use their foot to grasp food, which is then transferred to their beak.

Beaky Birds

Parrots have a tough, hooked beak. The beak is very effective at cracking open seeds and nuts, which make up a big part of the birds' diet.

The beak has other uses, too. Some parrots use the sharp point at the tip of the upper part of the beak to dig out juicy grubs—young insects —that live under tree bark. Parrots often use their beak like a third limb to hold onto branches and vines as they make their way through the thick vegetation of their forest home.

The inside of the beak contains the bird's jaws. The outside casing of the beak is made of a hard material called **keratin**. The bird's feathers and claws are also made of this material. Human fingernails and hair and the horns, fur, and hooves of many animals are made of keratin, too.

The keratin part of the beak never stops growing. The beak never gets too large because it is worn down with use. Even if the beak doesn't get enough wear from cracking open nuts, the parrot will file its beak against rocks or tree bark.

Body Basics

All parrots have a similar body shape. The head is rounded, the eyes are round, and the beak is curved. The head is joined to the stocky body by a short neck. The body is broad at the top and narrows toward the tail. When a parrot's wings are folded, they look like broad shoulders. Some of the bulk in the upper part of the parrot's body is muscle. Parrots are strong fliers. They have big flight muscles to power their wings.

The upper part of a parrot's legs is covered in small feathers. The lower part is featherless and covered in scales, just like the scales on reptiles. (Some scientists believe that birds and reptiles share a common ancestor that lived more than 200 million years ago.) The parrot's feet have four toes, each with a sharp claw on the end. Two of the toes face forward and two face backward. That arrangement helps the parrot grip well when climbing in the trees.

The red-winged parrot of Australia is a medium-sized parrot, measuring 12½ inches (27 cm) from head to tail.

A macaw takes
time to arrange
its feathers.

14

Fine Feathers

One feature that all birds share is a body covered in feathers. No other type of animal has feathers. There are different kinds of feathers on different parts of a bird. And these different types of feathers have different roles.

Much of a parrots body and head is covered in small fluffy feathers called **down**. Those keep the bird warm. Down traps air and prevents body heat from escaping on cool nights. They can also be moved to help heat escape if the parrot gets too hot during the day.

The tips of some down feathers break off and crumble into a fine powder. Scientists think that this powder serves a protective purpose, repelling water and keeping the feathers dry. Because it rains almost everyday in tropical forests, a parrot would spend a lot of its day wet and soggy if its feathers were not waterproofed. A soggy parrot would soon catch a cold! These "powder down" feathers never stop growing, so the parrot is never short of the protective powder.

Flight Feathers

The feathers used for flying are stiff, long, and strong. As the parrot opens its wings the flight feathers spread out like a fan. The wings are somewhat narrow and pointed. That allows the parrots to fly fast and make sharp turns.

Tail feathers are also important for flying. Different species of parrots have different tail lengths. Most use their tails as a rudder, to steer when they are in flight. Some parrots use their tail to slow them down as they land. They spread out their feathers, in the same way that a parachute slows a fall.

Other feathers, called **contour feathers**, give the bird a streamlined shape, so it cuts through the air with little resistance.

A scarlet macaw from Central America fans its tail as it comes in to land.

Rainbow lorikeets are also called "honey eaters." These parrots prefer to eat flowers, nectar, and pollen.

Amazing Colors

One of the most noticeable characteristics of parrots is their beautiful colors. Some parrots, such as the solitary lory, eastern rosella, or rainbow lorikeet, have feathers of four or more colors. Common colors for parrots include dazzling reds, vibrant yellows, electric blues, metallic greens, and zesty oranges. Parrots feathers can scatter light—that means that light can bounce off them to make the feathers appear to be a mixture of similar colors.

One of the dullest parrots is the African gray, which has grayish white **plumage**. However, this bird isn't completely drab—it has bright red tail feathers.

Colorful Camouflage

Many animals have dull colors or markings that allow them to blend into their surroundings. This kind of coloration is called **camouflage**. That way the animal can sneak up on prey unseen or remain invisible to predators. So why are parrots so colorful? Is it because no other animals eat them? Monkeys, snakes, and birds of prey, such as eagles and hawks, will attack and eat parrots given the chance.

The truth is that the parrots' bright plumage does actually camouflage them. The jungle home of parrots is very rich in colors. The **canopy** is full of exotic flowers and ripe colorful fruit. The leaves of the trees are many shades of vibrant greens. In addition, the sunlight that manages to penetrate the treetops dapples the leaves, creating more colors. Among the many hues and shades of the jungle, the parrots are nicely hidden from their enemies. Their colorful feathers look like leaves, flowers, or fruit against the tropical background.

The green feathers
of this orange-winged
Amazon parrot allow
the bird to blend in with
the leaves of trees.

Because of their amazing skills as a mimic, African grays have been popular pets for centuries.

Marvelous Mimics

Parrots, along with members of the crow family, are considered to be the most intelligent birds. A parrot's brain is large in comparison with the rest of its body and with other birds of similar size.

Parrots mimic sounds that they hear, including words and even whole sentences. They might even understand some of the words that they say. They will copy anything that they hear regularly, including a baby crying, a squeaky door, a noisy cat, or the ringtone of a phone. Parrots do not have vocal cords—which allow humans to speak. Parrots are actually whistling when they say words. The greatest mimic of all parrots is the African gray. Because pet parrots live for so long they might have quite a large vocabulary in their old age—up to 1,000 words!

In 1800, the explorer Alexander von Humboldt met an old parrot in South America that was the last remaining "speaker" of a native language. The tribe of Native South Americans who had kept the parrot had all since died.

Squawk to Me!

In addition to copying the sounds they hear, parrots have a not-so-endearing voice of their own. They make ear-piercing shrieks, squawks, and screeches. Many people who buy parrots as pets are soon annoyed by the natural noises that they make!

The parrots with the loudest squawks, such as macaws, usually live in thick forest. Their voices can carry far through the trees. That allows the birds to communicate with one another from a distance. It also helps a parrot easily find the rest of its **flock** if it gets separated.

Sight and Hearing

Parrots can see colors just like humans can. Some can even see ultraviolet, which humans cannot see. Color vision allows parrots to recognize one another easily in the thick forest. They also need color vision to tell colorful ripe fruit from unripe green fruit. If parrots could see only black and white and shades of gray it would be difficult for them to know which fruit to eat.

Hearing is the parrot's other most important main sense. They need sharp hearing to detect one another's calls when they can't see far through the thick jungle. Parrots don't have external ears like humans, cats, or dogs. Their ears are small slits on the sides of their head that are hidden by feathers. Although hidden, the ears can still hear very well.

There are a little more than 20 species of macaws—the biggest parrots. These blue-and-yellow macaws live in Central and South America.

Nuts and Seeds

Most parrots eat food from plants, such as nuts, seeds, fruit, berries, and occasionally shoots. For many parrots, nuts and seeds form the bulk of their diet. They crush the cases of the nuts and seeds in their tough beak and use their flexible tongue to pick out the softer insides. A parrot's beak is very strong—it has no problem breaking a hard nutshell, such as that of a Brazil nut.

Many nuts and seeds contain poisons. Parrots, however, have a clever way to avoid becoming ill. They eat small amounts of clay. In a parrot's guts, the minerals in clay filter out, or remove, the poisons in the food.

An African gray
parrot enjoys
a tasty walnut.

Orchard farmers in Australia
see rainbow lorikeets as
a pest. Flocks of the birds
strip fruit trees of their
flowers and fruit.

Not Just Nuts

Not all parrots eat nuts and seeds. The dazzlingly colorful lories and lorikeets of Australasia, Indonesia, and New Guinea prefer nectar and pollen, which they get by eating flowers. Nectar is the sweet sugar-water produced by flowers. Pollen are sticky grains that flowers produce in order to make seeds with other flowers of the same kind. Lories and lorikeets have a beak that is more slender than that of nut-crushing parrots. These nectar-feeders have a tongue with a brush on its tip to lap up the sweet liquid.

Other parrots sometimes eat slugs, water snails, and grubs that live under the bark of trees. Some parrots, such as cockatoos, even dig in the earth for juicy fat roots.

Cockatoos

Some zoologists, or scientists who study animals, classify cockatoos and cockatiels within the parrot family, Psittacidae (SI-TUH-SI-DAY). Others give them their own family, Cacatuidae (KA-KA-CHEW-I-DAY).

The most prominent feature of cockatoos—which sets them apart from other, or true, parrots—is their movable headcrest. Cockatoos have other differences, too. Their skull bones and the arrangement of their blood vessels are slightly different from other parrots. Cockatoos aren't as colorful as other parrots—they don't have the bright green and blue feathers that many parrots have. In addition, cockatoos have a limited range. They occur naturally only in Australia, New Guinea, Indonesia, and other islands in the South Pacific.

Cockatoos raise their
headcrest when they
are excited or alarmed.

Keas have a taste for rubber. They will peck at the rubber on the outside of cars, including windshield wipers and tires!

Keas and Kakapos

Six parrot species live in New Zealand, including two very interesting parrots: the kea and kakapo. The kea is an olive-green parrot with orange underwings and a long beak. Unlike other parrots, the kea will eat meat. One of its favorite meals is dead animals—called **carrion**—including sheep!

The kakapo cannot fly. It has mossy green feathers, with yellow feathers around the head. It also has whiskers around its beak, which are used to feel the ground as it walks. It is the heaviest parrot, weighing up to 4½ pounds (2 kg) and measuring 25 inches (64 cm) long. These fat birds are active at night and have **adapted** to climbing trees, walking, and jogging. There are fewer than 100 kakapos alive today. They all live on a protected island off New Zealand that is free of predators, such as rats, stoats, and cats. The bird is easy to catch. It freezes when danger is around and its very fragrant smell—like honey and lavender—gives it away. These parrots are also said to be very affectionate around people, acting more like a pet dog or cat than a bird!

All in a Day's Work

Parrots like to hang around together in flocks. The birds in the flock usually wake up before dawn and begin calling to one another with squawks and screeches. This deafening chorus lets all the birds know that each member of the flock is well and present.

Parrots like to keep their feathers in tiptop condition by grooming, or **preening**, themselves. When they are happy with their tidied feathers, the birds fly off to look for food. The birds land on a tree heavy with seeds, nuts, or fruit and feed until they are full. After eating, the birds might descend to the forest floor to search for more food or to find water to drink or bathe in. By now, the Sun is high in the sky so the parrots might look for somewhere shady to rest. The birds feed again in the cooler evening. As the Sun sets, the birds settle down for the night and gradually quiet down before falling asleep in their treetop **roosts**.

A bird with dirty or matted feathers cannot fly properly. That's why parrots spend a lot of time grooming themselves.

37

Male and female parrots —such as this pair of breeding blue-and-yellow macaws—generally look the same.

Pairing Up

Adult parrots pair up for the breeding season. Some, such as macaws and the parrots of the Amazon, pair up for life. However, they will seek another **mate** if one of them dies.

Parrots are very affectionate to their mates— they often kiss and rub each other's neck. They sleep at night pressed together. Lovebirds are so named because the male and female spend a lot of time preening each other. Pet parrots can be very affectionate, too. Some people believe that a pet parrot sees its owner as its mate!

The eclectus of northern Australia and New Guinea is an unusual parrot because the male and female look very different from each other. The male has green feathers and a yellow beak, and the female is red with a black beak. Zoologists originally thought they were two different species.

Nesting Holes

Most parrots are cavity nesters. That means that rather than building a nest out of sticks and twigs and lining it with soft moss and grass, they lay their eggs and raise their young in rough holes. They find holes in trees or among their roots, in the ground, or among rocks. Sometimes they take over abandoned holes made by other animals. They might also dig out a new hole, using their strong beak. Many parrots even make nesting holes in termite mounds—the insects try to defend their home by squirting a sticky substance at their unwanted guests. But the parrots don't seem to mind! Eventually the termites stop using the part of the mound where the parrots live.

Some parrots nest together in large groups called **colonies**. Monk parakeets build nests that are joined to other monk parakeets' nests by vines and branches. Together, all the nests are like an apartment building with each nesting pair having its own room.

A pair of Senegal
parrots look
around outside
their nesting hole.

These are the eggs of the echo parakeet, a parrot that was almost extinct in the 1980s. The bird has now bounced back as a result of a breeding program.

White Eggs

Depending on the species, female parrots lay between one and ten eggs. The female lays one egg every other day. Parrots' eggs are round and pure white. Many other types of birds lay speckled eggs that are camouflaged and, therefore, invisible to egg-eating predators. However, because parrots hide their eggs in holes, the eggshells don't need any markings to camouflage them.

The female sits on the eggs to keep them warm. That is called **incubation**, and it helps the young birds to develop in their egg. The young birds, or chicks, in unincubated eggs would soon die. The male brings the female food while she incubates the eggs. Some parrot pairs, such as cockatoos, take turns keeping the eggs warm.

Happy Hatchday!

Parrots' eggs hatch about three weeks after being laid. When the chicks hatch they are helpless, blind, and do not have feathers. They look like baby dinosaurs. Within a few days, the young birds can see and they grow soft, fluffy grayish-white down. A nesting hole can be very busy with fast-growing chicks of different ages all wanting to be fed. Both parents are kept busy bringing food to their chicks.

Depending on the type of parrot, the chicks stay in the nesting hole for up to three months. They lose their baby feathers and replace them with a full set of adult feathers. Once they grow their adult feathers, the young birds are equipped to fly. They soon follow their parents out of the nesting hole and practice flapping their wings. Their first flight might be a little difficult, but in no time they are expert fliers, just like their parents.

At about 50 days old, this echo parakeet chick is just beginning to grow adult feathers.

A rose-ringed parakeet
returns to its nesting hole
to feed its hungry chicks.

Almost Adults

Though now able to fly, the young parrots still need their parents to feed them. It might be a few months before they are fully independent. The young birds still have a lot to learn. They watch their parents and other members of the flock feed and groom themselves, and they copy. The young birds also learn what the different kinds of squawks mean.

Young parrots spend a lot of time playing. By pushing one another off branches, the young birds learn how to defend themselves and also how to balance, using their feet and sometimes beak to grab branches to steady themselves. By chasing one another through the air, the birds learn to make sharp turns. That might one day come in useful if they are pursued by a predator. These skills improve the chances that the young parrots will lead a long life in the wild and raise many families of their own.

Parrots in Peril

About one-quarter of parrot species is under threat. In recent years some, such as the Cuban macaw, have become extinct. The illegal pet trade is responsible for the death of thousands of parrots each year. The birds are trapped in the wild, but many do not make the adjustment to a life in captivity and die. Many of these birds die of a disease called psittacosis (SI-TUH-KO-SUS), which can spread to humans. In many countries, it is now against the law to trade, import, or export wild parrots.

Other parrots are dying as a result of the loss of their habitat due to **deforestation**. In addition native peoples often kill parrots for their feathers or for food. However, there is hope for parrots. Breeding programs exist for some parrots that are now extinct in the wild. In other places, forests are now protected and the parrots can live and breed without the threat of losing their home and source of food.

Words to Know

Adapted   Become better suited.

Breeding season The time of the year when animals
                     of the same kind mate.

Camouflage   Coloring or markings that allow
                     an animal to blend into its
                     surroundings.

Canopy   The treetop part of a forest.

Captivity   Not in the wild—raised by humans.

Carrion   Dead animals.

Colonies   Large groups of parrot pairs
                     nesting in the same location.

**Contour   Feathers on a bird's body that give
 feathers**   the bird a streamlined shape.

Deforestation   The cutting down of forest.

Down	Tiny, soft fluffy feathers.
Extinction	When a species of animal or plant no longer exists.
Flock	A group of parrots.
Incubation	Keeping eggs warm so the chicks grow and develop inside.
Keratin	A tough substance that makes up a bird's beak, claws, and feathers.
Mate	Either member of a breeding pair; to come together to produce young.
Plumage	Another word for feathers.
Predators	Animals that hunt other animals for food.
Preening	Cleaning and arranging feathers.
Roosts	Places to sleep, usually in a tree.

Find Out More

Books

Leon, V. *A Rainbow of Parrots*. Jean-Michel Cousteau Presents. Montrose, California: London Town Press, 2006.

Wexo, J. B. *Parrots*. Zoobooks. Poway, California: Wildlife Education, Ltd, 2001.

Web sites

African Gray Parrot
www.enchantedlearning.com/subjects/birds/printouts/Grayparrotprintout.shtml
Facts about the African gray with a picture to print and color in.

Parrot
animals.nationalgeographic.com/animals/birds/parrot.html
Information about parrots.

Index